JESUS IN THE HOOD

Jesus in the Hood

Charles E. Pender, Ph.D.

Library of Congress Control Number: 2018913768
ISBN: Hardcover 978-1-9845-6032-2
Softcover 978-1-9845-6031-5
eBook 978-1-9845-6030-8

Print information available on the last page.

Rev. date: 11/19/2018

To order additional copies of this book, contact:
Xlibris
1-888-795-4274
www.Xlibris.com
Orders@Xlibris.com
785755

Foreword

This spellbinding book, which is now served in your conscience, has glued you to your seat, wondering about a series that helps with a growing problem in the hood as to go forward as a series. This book will attempt to expose, under the guidance of the Holy Ghost, problems in the hood despite the historical information that you receive in this book, which will be indelibly imprinted on your mind. The main theme of this book is how we as a people can respect and treat one another as we've been so "Simonized" by society that we have lost our way. As is, our only recourse is to condemn the main story and to belittle one another, especially if we have a label like "down in the hood." The society we live in gives us labels and nothing in return,

Another descriptive term to make it was that it was so much a part of us, until we would become like crabs in a barrel. As you read this spellbinding book and listen to it in intricate detail, you have a choice at the end of the story to either be guilty but grateful to make a choice of being a fan of Simon or to be a fan of the prostitute—the hoe, the lot lizard, the soul sister in need. You can be the apostle of the demonized Simon and be very caustic in nature, or be very humble like the prostitute. It is up to you after you have read this book.

Experience and feel the touch of the Holy Ghost. The workbook in the back is designed just for you to help bring you into consciousness. And consciousness will give you hope. My sincerest desire is that after completing this book, you'll go back into the "hood," if you're not already in the hood, and practice the good legion of the Lord all day, every day, anywhere, and everywhere. Even there, you will find that Jesus is awaiting to forgive. Don't forget to renew, to encourage, and to enrich in the "hood," and to forgive and forget in the "hood."

From the beginning of civilization, Africans have had a great deal to do with shaping of the course of world history. Henceforth, the Garden of Eden, which the *Bible* states was located on the continent of Kamet (meaning the land of black face) and or what the Egyptians called AFRU-IKA, meaning motherland. The legendary name stems from Hannibal of Carthage who was an African general. This soul brother was born in 347 B.C. in the Bay of Tunis in North Africa, a city with a population at the time of a million Africans. Hannibal had the reputation of being one of the greatest military strategists and leaders of all time. Africa itself is named after a black Roman general, Scipio Africanus, who defeated Hannibal. The date of the defeat was October 19, 202 B.C. Thus, during creation, Adam and Eve were created in the Garden of Eden somewhere in Africa (Genesis 2:10–15).

Note: All *humans on the planet earth have African DNA.* We, all of mankind, have African DNA. That Y gene links us all to the African Adam; we are all 99.9 percently identical. The fact is, in a three billion base combined spectrum, and having 3,500 genes that determine our characteristics, only ten of those matches have to do with skin color. In other words, we are all joined at the hips in the hood here on planet earth. Our Heavenly Father created us all in His image, and all that He made was good (Genesis 1:18). Man was made in the image of God. Thus, all mankind are blessed (Genesis 1:28). And whatever and whomever God blesses, no man can curse (Genesis 5:2) (Acts 17:24–28). The only reason humans are on planet earth is to glorify our Father with our unique gifts which we were blessed with before we entered our mother's womb (Jeremiah 1:5, Psalm 139:13).

Note: Adam and Eve were blessed and made perfect. They did not need a tanning bed, eyeliner, lipstick, or blush to give them color; they were Africans! They were full-blown Africans with blessings of the sun and with skin rich in melanin given from God himself. They did not have any mutated genes. Their pineal glands were not calcified. Neither did they need hot curlers or Botox. They did not have any skin disorders. They were made perfect!

However, in that perfect Garden of Eden somewhere in Africa, Adam and Eve sinned by disobeying our Heavenly Father and were forced out of the perfect place. Later, as you read in Genesis, one of their sons named Cain slew his brother Abel. Mankind, afterward, multiplied and became so evil that God caused a great flood to get rid of the growing wickedness. But before the flood, Noah found favor in the *eyes* of the Lord. Noah, his wife, and three sons, Shem, Ham, and Japheth, along with their wives—a total of eight people—were spared and given directions by our Heavenly Father to build an ark. Noah and his family were spared because of this. But let us leave the story of Noah and deal with some facts before we go into the hood with Jesus.

Facts before We Go into the Hood

Fact: Readers must allow the *Bible* to speak for itself. Infer nothing or anything into it; just read it and pray, and then allow the Holy Ghost to make the *Word* very plain to its readers. Fact: Pictures were not used in the scroll *Bible* as the transcribers did not change the Word. The oppressors put pictures into the *Bible*, which were very misleading to many, even until today!

Some Facts You Should Know

Ham's people of North Africa were building the sphinx and pyramids centuries before the Europeans had established their government.

Fact: Some European governments were patented after the African government before Europeans learned to read or write.

Fact: The lovely Cleopatra of Egyptian fame, with all her captivating charm, was paper-sack brown and no different in appearance to the equally charming beauty of many true soul sisters of today.

Aesop, who lived in 560 B.C., did much to influence Western civilization by thought and morals. The word *Aesop* means Ethiopia or black. The impact of this man's genius was reflected in the thinking of Socrates, Plato and Shakespeare.

Fact: Solomon was the great king of Israel who built the temple on Mount Moriah 1,004 years before *Jesus* the Messiah. The cost to build the temple today would be in the amount of $5 million dollars. Solomon was a soul brother and a person of color. Solomon's mother, Bathsheba, was a Hittite from the clan of Ham (Genesis 10:15). She was a true soul sister.

Fact: Solomon said with his boldness, "Look not upon me because I am black, but comely, the word *comely* means good-looking from Regional account of people and also the dictionary... O ye daughters of Jerusalem." The question asked was, 'Was *Solomon* a player?' According to 1 Kings 11:3, Solomon had seven hundred wives and three hundred concubines. Of course he was a player in the hood. Solomon knew he was bodaciously handsome.

Solomon was not only handsome, but also blessed (Song of Solomon 1:5–6). The Queen of Sheba (a true soul sister), in her memorable visit from Ethiopia, exclaimed, referring to the glory of and grandeur of Solomon's court, that "the half has never been told." Solomon (a descendant of Canaanites) had ruled Israel in peace of splendor for 37 years. The Song of Solomon, Proverb, and Ecclesiastes were written by him.

Another fact to know is that the grandmother of Solomon's father, King David, was Ruth, a Moabite (Ruth 1:4, 4:13–22 and Nehemiah 13:23). And David himself was a soul brother. Check out his lineage in Matthew 1. David proceeded Martha and the Vandellas dancing in the street, humourously speaking. (2 Samuel 6:4). Some of the early writers of the *Bible* were African writers such as *Origen, Anthony and Athanasius*, the African dwarf who stood against the world to preserve the doctrine of the Trinity. The father of Western civilization was an African by the name of Augustine. Apostle Paul (Saul) was thought to be an Egyptian. He was from the tribe of Benjamin (Acts 21:38).

Here are more exciting facts!

Shakespeare's *Othello* was usually played by a dark person and was actually a Moor (Jeremiah 38:12). Often Celebrated men and scholars were sent to Europe from Numidia and Mauretania to be the part in these plays Facts Saint Augustine, possibly the world's greatest religious writer and teacher of ethics next to Saint Paul. Augustine was born in Numidia to an African mother and Roman father. He had a distinguished career as a writer and teacher in Italy and England before he returned to his home in Numidia where he died and was buried in A.D. 430.

Fact: Three Roman Catholic Church popes were of pure African blood:Pope Victor I, who brought about a large-scale conversion from paganism to the Catholic faith and established a unified time for easter for all nations; Pope Miltiades, who was credited with persuading Emperor Constantine to make Christianity the official religion of the Roman Empire; and probably the most remembered, Pope Gelacius I, who succeeded in having the Roman state acknowledge its lack of power over the church, thus establishing the principle of separation of church and state, so firmly adhered to today.

Hello. Let's see more amazing facts.

The *Bible* speaks for itself. It is our Father's Word through man. Just read it and pray. The Holy Ghost will reveal God's Word and make it plain. After the *Bible* was written, first by word of mouth, then by script and then later by press, note that no pictures were ever in the original versions until wickedness designed to influence people in a negative way were included. Pictures were not included in the original scroll *Bible* as the transcribers did not change the Word, but they put pictures, which were, until this day, misleading. This *fact* will *floor* you as we move closer into the hood.

The most infamous painting is that of Michelangelo's picture of Jesus. The replicas of the painting hang in millions of homes, churches and other places of note throughout the world, and what it depicts is far from the truth. Cesare Borgia's life is discussed in the book entitled, *A Triptych of Poisoners* and also in the book entitled, *Cesare Borgia: His Life and Times,* by Sarah Bradford. Between 1502 and 1503, he employed Leonardo da Vinci as a military architect and engineer. He and Leonardo da Vinci became intimate instantaneously; they were lovers. To express his love toward Cesare, Leonardo painted many pictures of him.

Cesare's father, Rodrigo Borgia, later became Pope Alexander. Under the authority of the Catholic Church elite, this pope had his son's picture put up as Jesus Christ in the Western world. Cesare had sex with his own sister Lucrezia and killed his brother Giovanni in 1497, and this was the man whom the Catholic Church gave their consent to to allow his picture to be put up and portrayed as Jesus Christ to deceive the whole world into thinking Christ was European.

See, what most people don't know is that there was a competition during the time called the Renaissance period. The competition was between Leonardo da Vinci and the well-known Michelangelo. The competition was to see who could impress the king by making a new image of the king's son that would deceive the world. Leonardo da Vinci won the competition. *Wow!* Did that fact knock you to your knees?

Here are more facts before we go into the hood.

The original *King James Holy Bible* in 1611 has the Apocrypha in it, but in 1928, the Vatican made an agreement to take fourteen books out of the *King James Holy Bible.* The Catholics, after thousands of years of research, found the true lineage of Christ. They found out that it was written in the wisdom of Solomon, located in the Apocrypha, and so knowingly, this was written in the wit and wisdom of Solomon.

The Roman Catholic Church took it out of the *Bible* so that people wouldn't know of their deception. It is a noted fact that when they did this, they knew exactly what Christ really looked like. They knew Christ and his people were not European, but instead were Hebrew Karma who were dark-brown people. So let's find out in the *Bible,* first, what Satan was going to do, and then we will find out what exactly was written in the wisdom of Solomon in the Apocrypha.

This was taken out and credited as unscripted and not divinely inspired by the Catholic Church. (This requires some research from you. Make sure you're sitting on the floor as the information you will get may knock you to your knees.) Here are further facts. The *Bible* was originally written on the *hood.* The language was Hebrew/ Aramaic.

The *Bible* itself in all of its themes, for example, the theatrics of war and everything happened on the continent of Africa. Fact is, there are no white people in the *Bible.* In fact, it is virtually impossible for them to have been in it. England had not yet been established. There were no blue-eyed blond-haired people. The fact is that the word about white people came in the late 1700s. Another fact is that our Father separated all of humanity by nation, tribes, clans, kindred and tongues. Satan appeared in the form of an anthropologist (Johann Blumenbach, the instigator) and others who diametrically opposed God by sanctioning *witchcraft*, which many people today call racism.

The Origin of Mankind after the Flood Facts

According to Genesis 9:19 and the Table of Nations in Genesis 10, all mankind is descended from the three sons of Noah: *Shem, Ham and Japheth.* (For some strange reason, Noah's sons are always listed in that order, although Genesis 10:21 says Japheth was Shem's older brother. Normally in the *Bible*, sons are listed in chronological order.)

The descendants of Japheth settled in *Anatolia*, modern-day Turkey, and from there, moved into the Caucasus Mountains of Western Russia and from there, settled in Europe and Russia. They are the ancestors of the Caucasian people. Their main impact on Israel was through the Persians, the Greeks and the Romans. Ham's descendants became the various black people who settled in the African continent and parts of the Arabian peninsula. His sons include Cush, whose descendants settled in Ethiopia, and Mizraim, father of Egypt, whose descendants settled in Palestine and founded the cities of Sidon, Tyre and Carthage and, among others, were the ancestors of the Phoenicians.

Collectively, in ancient times, the descendants of Cush formed a large ethnic group and were the main populace of the Cushite Empire, which extended from present-day western Libya to Ethiopia and Nubia, south of Egypt, all of present-day Egypt and the Arabian peninsula into the mountains of Turkey. They spoke a variety of languages and had skin pigmentation ranging from dark brown to medium brown.

One of Cush's sons was Nimrod, the mighty hunter who was the founder of Babylon, Akkad, Assyria and Nineveh—several of early mankind's most powerful nations and cities. Their languages are generally referred to as belonging to the Western Semitic group, although they actually are Hamitic. Mizraim's descendants became the Ludim, Anamim, Lehabim, Naphtuhim, Pathrusim and Casluhim (Philistines). According to the Jewish-Roman historian, Flavius Josephus, most of these peoples were destroyed in the Ethiopic War.

The Mythical "Curse of Ham" and the Actual Curse of Canaan

It is often claimed that Noah placed a curse on his son, Ham. Apparently, Noah had become drunk with wine and Ham "looked upon his father's nakedness." Some scholars interpret this as a euphemism and believe that Ham had homosexual intercourse with his father; others believe the reason for the curse was the disgrace Ham caused by telling others. In any event, Genesis 9:25–27 recorded that, in fact, Noah cursed Ham's youngest son, Canaan, not Ham [25]: he said, "Cursed be Canaan! The lowest of slaves will he be to his brothers." He also said [26], "Blessed be the LORD, the God of Shem! May Canaan be the Servant of Shem. [27] May God extend the territory of Japheth; may Japheth live in the tents of Shem, and may Canaan be his Servant."

Canaan's descendants founded Sidon and, among others, were the ancestors of the Jebusites, Amorites, Girgashites, Hivites, Arkites, Sinites, Arvadites, Zemarites and Hamathites. There is ample historical evidence that, indeed, they were cursed with moral depravity, including temple prostitutes and human sacrifice. One scholar, Lenormant, said the following of the Canaanite religion: "No other people ever rivaled them in the mixture of bloodshed and debauchery with which they thought to honor the Deity" (per summary of Near Eastern History, cited below.)

Jesus's Family of Color

Shem's descendants became the Semitic peoples who settled in parts of the Arabian peninsula, including what is now Saudi Arabia, Yemen, Jordan, Israel and Lebanon. They were of a generally medium-brown complexion with facial features roughly midway between typical Negro and typical Caucasian, and the languages they spoke included Arabic, Hebrew and Aramaic, Jesus's native language. It is important to realize that in Old Testament times, Egyptians were black, not Arabs. Arabs first conquered Egypt when Moslems invaded Egypt. This took place in the "Hood" after the death of Muhammad. The original Jews were people of color. Perhaps you would want to read history's accounts.

The center of the relationship with God is and always will be the Ten Commandments, which set high moral standards before God, and this is what the early Jews were equipped with before they entered the hood.

The Ten Commandments (Exodus 20:2–17 NKJV)

1. "I am the Lord your God, who brought you out of the land of Egypt, out of the house of bondage. You shall have no other gods before Me.
2. "You shall not make for yourself a carved image, or any likeness of anything that is in heaven above, or that is in the earth beneath, or that is in the water under the earth; you shall not bow down to them nor serve them. For I, the Lord your God, am a jealous God, visiting the iniquity of the fathers on the children to the third and fourth generations of those who hate Me, but showing mercy to thousands, to those who love Me and keep My Commandments.
3. "You shall not take the name of the Lord your God in vain, for the Lord will not hold him guiltless who takes his name in vain.
4. "Remember the Sabbath day, to keep it holy. Six days you shall labor and do all your work, but the seventh day is the

Sabbath of the Lord your God. In it, you shall do no work: you, nor your son, nor your daughter, nor your male servant, nor your female servant, nor your cattle, nor your stranger who is within your gates. For in six days the Lord made the heavens and the earth, the sea, and all that is in them, and rested the seventh day. Therefore the Lord blessed the Sabbath day and hallowed it.

5. "Honor your father and your mother that your days may be long upon the land which the Lord Your God is giving you.
6. "You shall not murder.
7. "You shall not commit adultery.
8. "You shall not steal.
9. "You shall not bear false witness against your neighbor.
10. "You shall not covet your neighbor's house; you shall not covet your neighbor's wife, nor his male servant, nor his female servant, nor his ox, nor his donkey, nor anything that is your neighbor's."

Here's one of the most interesting facts for your understand before we enter the Hood. The extermination of the Canaanites had everything to do with the righteous judgment of God our Father and nothing else. So what were the Canaanites doing that was so horrendous that it warranted their destruction? The nature of the Canaanites is one you must understand when we talk about the Sins and the practice of the Canaanites. We are not talking about a small group of people; we're talking about a nation. We are talking about everyone. Everyone, including women and, in some cases, children, was involved in and promoted idolatry, bestiality, child sacrifice and many other grotesque practices. The mythical curse as you know of Canaan gave people a bad name. It stems from the curse of Noah.

This curse was upon Canaan, but not Ham, who had committed the offense.

When Israel first ventured into the Promised Land (the hood), God sent two witnesses to give the people in Jericho an opportunity to repent and escape the impending judgment. You find this in Joshua in the 2nd chapter and James II first 25. As an example, remember Rahab the prostitute? She and her family repented, and they escaped the judgment and also became a part of Israel. In fact, Jesus's great-grandmother was Rahab. You find this in Matthew, the first chapter and the third verse. Before the Israelites were to enter into the badlands that is the hood called Canaan, He gave his people the Ten Commandments to remember them until this day or else they would be lost forever. God placed the holy code and prohibited them from worshipping false gods and other ball acts. Many centuries before Israel at the land of Palestine, ancient Canaanite fertility gods had sexual rituals to worship their false god.

God instructed Israel not to be involved in the practices of sexual fertility goddess and gods in Egypt. In other words, do not participate with the prostitute in the pagan worship of false gods.

God had warned against worshipping Moloch, the Canaanite fire god, and giving in to their religious context of believing the Jews living in the land of Israel. They were prohibited from pagan sexual worship of the Canaanite fertility goddess because God viewed such worship as an abomination.

Moloch was a Canaanite god that required child sacrifice. Moloch was portrayed as a man with the head of a bull sitting upright with his arms outstretched. Inside his stomach was fire, and a child would be placed in the arms and burned. Moloch required that you sacrifice your firstborn son to him in order to shore a blessing. Infant children as old as five were offered up to him. If you built a house, you were required to sacrifice one of your children as a cornerstone to the building to ensure that the gods would bless the house and the family and all their days. And if someone wanted a guaranteed victory in battle, they would sacrifice one of their children to ensure that god would fight on their behalf. Sexual acts, incest, adultery and all types of lewd acts were done openly in Canaan, the hood.

Canaan had temple prostitutes, both male and female, who had dedicated their bodies to the pagen gods. They were considered holy priests. People would go to the temple to have sex with these prostitutes as an act of worship. The people of ancient Canaan did sexual acts with the priests and with the pagan goddess herself. Sex is one of the most compelling forces on planet earth; it's like a raging bull in a China shop!

Before we go further into the hood, let's get some more very interesting facts about the lineage of Jesus from the book of Matthew. Jesus descended from the line of Shem. The records show that Abraham had sons, and one of the son's name was Judah.

Judah was the father of Perez and Zerah, whose mother was Tamar, a Canaanite, one of Ham's relatives. So now we see a connection between Shem and Ham intermarrying through this soul brother by the name of Perez. They had a son by the name of Salmon, who married the former prostitute Rahab. You do remember that back in the day, in the book of Joshua, apparently, all ladies of the evening looked good. They were good-looking prostitutes with black hair and lovely lips that were probably round and full. Their tongues probably tasted like a honeycomb. Their breasts stood up like taillights on a '59 Cadillac. These soul sisters were really saying something, butRahab turned over a new leaf and decided to follow God.

Rahab married Salmon, the great-grandson of Perez. Then came the birth of a soul brother by the name of Boaz, who fathered Obed.

His mother, Ruth, was a Moabite who was the mother of Jesse, and Jessie begot David, who was also a brother dancing in the street (2 Samuel 6:14). David was the father of Solomon, whose mother was the Bathsheba as you may recall. David had her husband killed; his name was Uriah. Uriah was a Hittite. These Hittites are Ham's in-laws from his clan, so now you have an identity of some soul brothers and soul sisters in Jesus's lineage. You can trace the lineage from Genesis 10.

We see that people in Jesus's family are varied and complicated, but we also see a family that can be forgiven and have in them the lineage of the savior of the world. All this happened in the hood. Remember, readers, God separated men by kindreds, nations, tribes, tongue and clans. Never in the *Bible* was the word *race* mentioned; the color of someone's skin did not matter. Only the relationship that each tribe, clan, nation, and tongue had with our Heavenly Father. As you read the modern *Bible*, which is a version of the Jewish bible about Jewish people, you learn who the father of modern Christianity is. It's all about a Jewish savior named Jesus, who was willing to save us all.

With this background, we are going on in and around the hood. Let us enter into it with an interesting scenario, a documented situation that happened in the life of Jesus, only it happened then, but it's also happening now. How can you handle this situation with a lot lizard who was willing to give up prostitution to get out? Her pimp was a wimpwho tried to put Jesus on the spot. We are going to the hood, and afterward, there are going to be some questions for you. I can assure you there will be a ton of answers to questions that folks are stressing over in an effort to survive day by day in the hood.

The story begins somewhere in the hood in Africa years ago as described by Robert Bob Lively, the author of this guilty but grateful episode found in the book of Luke, the 7th chapter verses 36 to 50. If you don't mind, turn to your neighbor and say, "Neighbor, I'm not innocent, but I am grateful."

We've all used labels that we stick on jackets and manila folders, CDs and DVDs so that we remember what's on the inside.

We stick them on people the same way because we think we know what's on their inside. But the problem with labels is that when it comes to people, they are meerly an assumption. People are multifaceted, complex and multidimensional, and when we apply labels to them, we put on blinders and see only a narrow view of what is an expensive, mysterious and complex human being. They are doing that one thing, but also many other things. All this is taking place in the hood.

When we are speaking to people, there is nothing wrong with using descriptive terms, but there is a big difference between descriptions and labels. Descriptions are based on fact, and labels are an attempt to reduce and the deduce somebody to a one-dimensional artifact of a profound person that they are not. This act is one of engaging in what I call the consumption of assumption. One consumes back what we assume to be right, whether it is or not. And when we label people, it is not only unfair, but also hurtful because in spite of the nursery rhyme that says, "Sticks and stones may break my bones, but words will never hurt me," somebody is a witness here that words can and do really hurt you (I know that's right!).

I'm looking for a few people who can testify today to the pain you felt when you were unfairly labeled by somebody else. They called you something that you knew you were not. They may have tagged you with a title that did not match your testimony. They designated you with a decal that was not compatible with your ultimate destiny. Let me go a little bit further. Is there anybody here who is honest enough to admit that you have have labeled somebody? (Okay now! Don't be lying up in here!) And before you ever met them, you had an opinion of them because you had already labeled them. Now what do we gain by okaying the labeling of others in the hood?

There are many reasons for this. I like to give you seven very quickly: 1) It is easier to require less effort to assume something is true rather than to work to find out the fact; 2) When we are uncertain of the fact, we often go along with what others (herd mentality) tell us rather than admit our ignorance; 3) It may be a hollow attempt to elevate one's own stature by demoralizing and ridiculing and trivializing somebody else because we erroneously believe that we can become taller by standing on them or over them; 4) We might be fearful, envious and suspicious of others; 5) We like critical thinking; 6) We may have been brought up to be biased and discriminatory, prejudiced and hateful; and 7) It may be simply the effort to try to control somebody else. But whatever the reason for labeling others, I want to affirm very pointedly that it is judgmental, and it is wrong. Say it's wrong, somebody in the hood, or anyplace else.

You see, labeling leads to stigma, a word that means "breaking and shame," and stigma leads to discrimination and all types of misfortune. It is wrong in our text for today. Jesus confronts our proclivity to label others and challenges us to overcome this by cultivating unconditional acceptance, compassion and understanding. Jesus challenges us each to step past a label and learn to love in the hood and everywhere else because, ultimately, the reason that it is so easy to label others is that it is easier to label them than it is to love them.

Let me give you a situation so that you can hopefully see the subject. Jesus was invited to the home of Simon, a Pharisee. Notice that he is named in the text so as to bring particular attention to his person. He is "somebody" whose name was not only known, but also closely associated with the group to which he belonged. He was a Pharisee. That was his pedigree, like being an lpha, or a Q, a Mmason, an Elk, a Democrat, or a Republican. His bag testified to who he was and where he was in that ancient community,

This was the man who invited Jesus to dinner. Simon, a notable name in the community, a mogul, a big baller, is the shot caller. And the homes of the rich and the famous at that time were constructed with open courtyards where the probing public were permitted to stand and overhear the conversations by the fluents and their influence. All this happened now in the hood.

Standing somewhere in the shoulder-pumping of the crowd that day was a wriggling sister who steped in to set this stage in the scripture. Now notice, her name was not known, nor was it mentioned. This is because she is presumably a "nobody," a nobody with no status, no class, no notable achievements and no commendable accomplishments. She wasn't nobody whose name was not known, and yet she was clearly identified with the group in which she had been assigned by the culture. Because she was not called a Pharisee, she was called a prostitute. That was her pedigree, like being called a hooker, a lot lizard, a hoochie mama or a skank, pusher or a pimp, or a thug or just a convict. Her tag testified to who she was and where she was in the ranking of that ancient society. That was the woman who decided in desperation that no courtyard eavesdropping would suffice for her that day; she needed to make contact with Jesus.

Driven by desperation, she pushed past the labels that others had placed on her life and on her experience. She knew the policy, protocol, practice and procedure for questions at this Pharisee's house. A designated stranger intrudes into the "decidedly sacred."

Come here inside *this* door for *this* moment because I need to encourage somebody listening to me today to *leap* past the labels that others have assigned to your life. Leap on past it. No matter what they say to you, no matter what they say about you, you are not inferior to anyone or anything in the hood or anywhere else.

Do not accept anyone's negative estimation or evaluation of who you are or what your life is about, where you're headed, or what God is going to do in your situation. Remember that if they cannot define you, they cannot confine you. You are not helpless, you are not hopeless, you are not dumb not dysfunctional depleted, defeated, or deleted. You are not second-class. You're a child of the king.

The struggling sister leaped past the label placed on her that was designed to limit her and made contact with the Christ. Her intruding presence was intolerable because her jk condition was unacceptable in the minds of those so-called holy folks who were gathered in the house. Her place as a woman with a questionable résumé and a stained past was outside in the dark, on the down low on the corner. But the strong sister, driven by desperation, would not permit the labels that everyone had placed on her to keep her from the only one who could help her and change her. Her desperation was greater than her activation. So with determination, she pressed her way into the presence of Jesus.

Can I pull up in your driveway today just for a moment? I believe that this struggling sister with a label on her life has something significant to teach us about the effects of gratitude in the human heart.

How do you know that you are truly grateful? The first way is to know you are not passive. Say *passive*. See, Simon invited Jesus to dinner, but was perfectly passive about extending to him any hospitality. We know that he invited him, but was really not clear as to why he had done so. Based on his reaction in verse 39, Simon did not appear to be a follower of Christ nor did he appear to think much of Jesus because he treated him with cool contempt. Common courtesy in that day, at that time, was to greet your guests not with a handshake, but with a kiss. And I'm not anointing the head with olive oil and washing the dust from the hot, tired feet. Not only did Simon fail to do any of that for Jesus, but the apparent absence of what was considered common courtesy and common hospitality suggests that there was an underlying animosity for Jesus on the part of Simon. He was a hater of the down low, and I need to stop here long enough to tell you that not everybody who invites you anwhere is really interested in you. Not everyone around you is actually for you. Some people only want to know you because they are hoping to dismiss you, reduce you, or replace you.

Simon carefully avoided every custom that would have made Jesus feel welcome. One can only assume that he was the kind of person who tried to impress people by hobnobbing with known celebrities: the type of person who wanted to be known by whom they know. But Jesus accepted Simon's invitation, although he detected this human weakness. In fact, His power and love were so ubiquitous and comprehensiveness to Simon all that day and is will be forever in the hood and elsewhere.

Jesus practiced what I call "radical inclusiveness." It's a willingness to reach out to anybody and everybody, and although Simon treated Jesus passively, this struggling sister in the scripture did not. Gripped by regret and hopelessness, and overcome by emotions and convictions, she pressed her way to Jesus' presence and fell at his feet in tears. Somebody needs to know that when a person understands that they really need God, that is because they hat they have come to the point where they can no longer ask for admission ; they no longer seek validation, and they no longer need to confirm whether or not what they are doing is right. They do whatever they have to do in order to get to God.

Say I have a witness up in here somewhere. Amen! You see, in sharp contrast to self-righteousness and the self-righteous Simon, she pushed her way through the outer core. She scrambled past the security trying to get to Jesus. She had heard through the grapevine that Jesus was a friend of sinners, and based on her résumé, she was well qualified in that department. *Criticized or not, I must get to Jesus*, and when her eyes fixed that focus on Him, all the other guests faded in the midst of tears.

Suddenly, it didn't matter what the educated, the elite, or the sophisticated said about her. Her only thoughts were about only seeing Jesus. I'm going to help you right here because there's a dose of medicine that all of us need to take before the benediction of this book. Before we leave the church today (your church could be on the street corner or at a bar, on the beach, or anywhere else) and go into the hood, as you read this sermon, Wherever it might be, look at the back of the church, which is the back of *this* book, for some homework so you can meet Jesus every day. Let us be more compassionate. Be like Jesus in the hood.

You see, the reason why people go to church every weekend and still are depressed and discouraged, disillusioned and disenchanted is because they focus on everything and everybody but Jesus. Can I get a witness in here to grab the phone and tell your neighbors put your eyes on Jesus? Tell your friends to put their eyes on Jesus. You see, all that this prostitute saw was Jesus. She was not passive. She understood that if she was going to be delivered, it was going to take something on her part. Her notoriety was well established in that ancient neighborhood, but her girlfriends downtown at the beauty shop had told her between a manicure and a pedicure about Jesus's gracious invitation. "Come unto me all ye that labor and are heavy laden, and I will give you rest."

She knew that she needed him. Is it true that anybody here that's reading this book might need Him today? You may be in church now or even sitting at your house; wherever you are, you're in church now. Is there anybody here in the service that know if they need Jesus? I need Him to be so many different reasons and so many different ways every single day.

With labels not limiting her progress and restricting her advancement, she actively demonstrated her reverence for Jesus and leaped past the labels and got into his presence, obviously to the glaring critical looks of the bystanders. She got in his presence with the hope of giving him her most prized possession—a box of alabaster oil. She was not passive, but she was actively humble. Tell your neighbors that humility is a necessary prerequisite for the grace of God.

If you want God to elevate you, you have got to understand that the way up is first down. The *Bible* says, "Humble yourself before the mighty hand of God, and in due season, he will exalt you." God never elevates anyone who is stuck on themselves. When you humble yourself in the sight of God and bring yourself low, then grace is on its way because the *Bible* says that the Lord is near to those who are of a contrite heart and save those of a broken spirit (Psalm 34:18).

She was actively humble. She was not passive. How do you know that you're truly grateful? Well, you're past it because, watch this, you know that you are not perfect. (Somebody should say "Amen" right there.) But let me clarify something. None of us have ever met a perfect person, and none of us are perfect people. Some of us think we are, but we are not. No, you're not. Thomas Wilson said, "The greatest of all disorders is to think that you're whole and need no help." That's why Paul wrote in Romans 12:3, "Through the grace given to me, I said to everyone of you not to think of yourself more highly than you ought to think, think soberly according as God has given to each of you a measure of faith." Touch your neighbor, and say, "You wouldn't be anything without God. Amen."

Billy Graham once said, "The smallest package ever seen was a man wrapped up in himself." None of us have ever met a perfect person, and none of us are perfect people. If you don't believe that, then believe when Romans 3:10 says there is none righteous. No, not one. Please tell your neighbors not no one.

Romans 3:23 says, "For all have sinned and come short of the glory of God." Tell your neighbors all but here the shocking material. You don't have to be perfect in order to be blessed, in order to be a favorite, in order to be healed, in order to be elevated, in order to be grateful. Henceforth, in this, we get a glimpse of the incarnation of God in Christ and how that God identifies with a lost, the least, the little, the looked over and the last. John 3:16 says, "For God so loved the world that he gave his only begotten son that whosoever believeth in him should not perish but have everlasting life." Touch your neighbor and say, "I'm in that crowd in the hood."

Jesus practiced radical wellness to include and to receive those who were deemed "socially, racially, morally and spiritually unacceptable." Somebody ought to shout "Hallelujah" right now because it does not matter who reject you. I want you to know in no uncertain terms that Jesus died on the cross for you. Don't let somebody else's label block you from the love that God is trying to give you. You are to turn to somebody with an attitude and say, "God loves me, and you ain't got to be like me. You ain't got to validate me. You ain't got to understand me. You ain't got to talk to me. All you have to do is appreciate me. You can just sit there like a bump on a log, but I'm still going to be blessed in Jesus's name." let the church shout "Hallelujah" this is what happens when Jesus includes us.

Universities and graduate schools cater to the intellectual elite and have no patience with slow learners, flow scorers and late bloomers. In this culture, it is easier to be excluded. If you live in the wrong neighborhood, if you drive a hooptie, if you don't work for minimum wages, it's easy to be excluded. And that's not only true in the culture or in the community. It is also true in the church. If you don't hang with the right group, if you don't kick it with the right crew, if you don't speak the right tongue, if you don't poke the right verse, if you don't drive the right car, if you don't live in the right neighborhood, if you're not in the clique, if you don't have the right title, if you don't make the right money, you are subject to be excluded in the house of God—amen—even in the hood.

You see, unlike Simon, Jesus knew that this woman was not perfect. Simon was not grateful for the presence of Christ because he sensed no need for Christ. He thought that he was alright. *I'm good enough. I come to the eleven o'clock service every week. I even return my tithe and offering and do nothing on the holy day. I meet the church's standards. I'm in with the in-crowd. I do not drink. I don't smoke. I don't associate with those that do. In fact, I don't eat the kind of food that they eat. You ain't got nothing left to do but to die.* You see, Simon felt justified looking down his self-righteous nose at this struggling sister because the culture called her a prostitute. The culture called her a sinner because they had no need for Christ. Who knew where that whore's hand had been?

I'm sorry, y'all, but there's a problem in this text. I got two issues with Simon. Can I share them with you? Here's the first one: how did Simon know that she was a hoe? And why was she so familiar with his house? I'm sorry. That's another sermon for another day. Touch somebody and say you don't want to go down that road.

Now my second problem is Simon's logic. His logic was based on false assumptions, so it could only leave false conclusions in the hood. Simon assumed that withholding love and appreciation would lead to separation. He failed to realize that separation doesn't always mean no sanctification. Jesus knew the woman's character, but he also knew Simon's. See, we always want God to judge, evaluate, critique and straighten out other people, but God wants us to know that it is not *only* other people. who need straightening out. Somebody here today please say, "Sir, please, ma'am, be careful before you judge somebody else. You don't know what they have been through. You don't know how they're struggling. You don't know the tears they had to share." The next time you see somebody on the ground, don't assume that they are no good. You don't know how long they were standing before they finally fell down, and you would be in the same place if it were not for the grace of God.

Simon was self-righteous, but not that woman. That woman was guilty, but she knew that she needed the grace of God. I don't know about you, but I need grace every day. I need grace today. I'm going to need grace tomorrow. I'm going to need the grace the day after tomorrow. I'm going to continue to have grace because I realized His grace and mercy brought us through. We are living in this moment because of the blood of Jesus shed for me, my brothers and sisters, and you. Is there anyone reading this book who can say, "I know I need grace. I know I need mercy. I'm not whole"? How do you know when you are truly grateful? You're not passive because you're not perfect, but also, you're not pretending. Look at somebody and say, "I'm real with mine." You see, there was nothing phony about her praise. There was nothing artificial about her adoration. This sister was real.

She came in desperation and adoration, and humiliation created a complication because her grace became an irritation for Simon. Why? Because Simon was faking, and whenever someone is faking and they run across somebody who isn't, it's going to be a problem. See, one of the greatest problems of the church in the hood is plastic people who sometimes show up at church. We get too many people with false eyes, false hair, false teeth, false nails and a false personality looking for a *real* relationship. Only in Christ will you find a real, genuine relationship.

She was real with herself. Look, it's right there in the text, and the way you know that Simon was not real and just faking is that you got to remember now who invited Jesus in the first place: Simon! You got that. You do not expect to be invited to someone's house and then be insulted. Y'all don't hear me. Usually, people who invite you to their home or anywhere want you around. Am I making sense?

Look at verse 39 where Simon reveals his true self. He says if Jesus were a prophet, He would know what type of woman it was who touched Him. If He would have known her past, if He were a prophet, He would part company with her. If He were a true teacher, He wouldn't let her touch him that way. Now for this service today, I'd like to make it plain what Simon really wanted to say, but he didn't know how to say it. So I'm going to say what he wanted to say. "I wouldn't let that hoe put her hands on me." I pray that y'all don't handle it like that in the hood.

If you notice, Simon's logic was based on false assumptions. This led to a false confession that Simon assumed happened. He failed to realize that separation doesn't always mean happiness. Jesus knew the woman's character, but he also knew Simon's.

That woman was guilty, but she was grateful. She was not concerned about the hypocrites around her. She worshipped Jesus right then and there. You never truly worship until you worship Him. I'm surrounded by hypocrites. Somebody thank Jesus for the hypocrite. I want us to worship Jesus right now. See, a whole lot of us are working on and praying for, and have some idea of a perfect environment, for everybody's going to be on one accord soon. Everybody is going to be like one another. You will not even find a church service like this nowhere on the planet earth. But if you worship God, you can get to be like this woman. She is saying, "I'm not concerned about what you're saying about me," with tears running down her face, snot running out her nose, and disshevled hair. She said she still going to worship Him.

You worship whatever or whoever is in your heart. Many folks worship people more than they workshop God. We sometimes don't know their names or the team on TV and they are not going to pay the bills, but you give them more praise than you give to God who woke you up this morning.

Let's give God the praise that we woke up this morning. This woman said, "Christ—I want to worship Him. I know I'm not looking churchified today. I don't even have a towel to dry His feet, so let me use my dreads." You know this is the true meaning of worship. She was at His feet worshipping, and it was ugly. Turn to your neighbor. She said it was ugly so she lost herself at his feet. Have that ever happened to you? See, we're in a praise generation. Everything is "Praise God, praise Him, praise Him, praise Him, praise Him." Nobody loves to praise God more than I do. I love to praise God and His Holy name. He is my rock, my sword, my shield. He's my wheel in the middle of a wheel. I love to praise him. You know that, don't you? But here's the problem in our praise. It is based upon what He does for us.

So I come to church and just got a job. "Lord, I want to thank you. I want to thank you for my new clothes and my new shoes and my new job. You know that I was wasn't really qualified, but oh, I want to thank you and praise you because you gave me favor in the interview or you moved my new location to the top of the file. You allowed them to like me when there were so many others to like. And I got the job even though I didn't deserve the job. So since I got the job, Lord; it isn't paying as much, but I still want to praise you."

See? Now, worship is not focusing on what God *did*; it is focusing on what God *is* and *who* He is so that you learn to worship God. You know what? Start *praying* that you don't get the job. If I don't get the promotion, if my words break down, if I have to shop at Walmart for the rest of my life, if I have to eat hot dogs now, if I had to eat sausage links and vegetarian bean stew just to survive, if my man doesn't come back, if my woman walks out on me, if I have to drive a hooptie or a Bentley, it does not matter. I'm still going to bless the Lord because He's worthy to be praised.

Now I got to worshippers in here. See, I know how to tell the difference. When you are just a person who prays, you can try to do it where people are worshipping, that is, in church, because people praise when there's an audience. But worshipping can be at home while washing the dishes or washing the car or washing a dog. Just think how you were saved by the blood of Jesus. You may throw soap suds in the air because they you what Jesus did for you in the hood.

How do you know when you are grateful? You are not passive because you're not perfect. You are not pretending, but here's the raw material. You are not prohibited because notice that Simon was irritated, but Jesus did not turn him away. Jesus looked at Simon and said, "Simon, I have something to say to you." And he told him the story about two debtors (Luke 7:40-49). One had a lot of debt and the other only a little, but neither of them was able to pay off the debt, so both of them had that debt to pay. Jesus said, "Who will be more grateful?"

Simon said, "I suppose the one who was forgiven the most." And Jesus said, "You have answered correctly." Then he went on to point out the sinner's lack of spirituality while turning his back to His host and His face toward the woman. Now this is for all the worshippers because that's what worship gets you.

Worship gets you FaceTime with God. (You'll get that later.) But let's continue with the story. Jesus was still addressing Simon, but his back was to him now. With his body language, Jesus demonstrated His acceptance of the story because She had done what Simon refused to do. She is coming to Jesus with her sins of admission and her sins of commission." Simon thought that he was perfect. She knew that she was not. She was a sinner, but so was Simon because there were only two types of sinners in the world, and everybody here fits into one of those categories. You, the reader, also fit into a category. There's some who know they are sinners, and there are those who think they are not. The only difference is awareness.

They were with debtors, but this woman was aware of her sins. So she came to Jesus out of love, seeking forgiveness. She was a sinner, but the Lord did not turn her away because God is not so much entertained about where you've been as to where you're going. She was not prohibited. She was permitted. She was given success, and Jesus turned to the woman that had come in desperation and demonstration with adoration, moving from desperate and irritation, and gave her an explanation that was an elevation. He said, "Girl, your sins are forgiven. Hallelujah, your faith has saved you. Go in peace." That's good news for all of us in here today and for all of us reading this book today, and if you come to God in humility and honesty, the Lord is willing to forgive you no matter what you've done or failed to do.

Jesus has a love that is large enough, a mind that is responsive enough, a heart that is wholly enough, and a grace that is compassionate enough and comprehensive enough to include everybody at any time and any place.

Yes, this incident took place in the hood then and is happening even now. But just as then and now, Jesus has his hands out to forgive us for our sins. It is available for men, it's available for women, it is available for the strong, it is available for the weak, it is available for the straight, it is available for the gays, it is available for the saints, it is available for the saints, it's available for the educated, it's available to the upper class, it's available to the middle class, it's available to the lower class, it's available for the ain't-got-nothing class, it is available to the MD, it's available to the Ph.D., it's available to the JDs, it's available to the GED, it's available to the ain't got no D. Forgiveness is available to those who think they are something and those who know they're not the thugs and trumps, the pimps and pushers, the hustlers and the hoes.

I am here today to ask you, who you will side with: Simon or the hoe? I side with the hoe every time because she was willing and she was grateful. She was not innocent. Jesus saved her from the gutter MOs to the outermost. I wonder if there's anybody here who can praise God just because he saved you, just because he rescued you? You can look at yourself and look at your neighbor and say, "I'm not perfect. I'm not innocent, but I am grateful. Praise the Lord in the hood."

Following is a workbook and tutorials on how you can strengthen your faith, how you can increase your spiritual growth in the hood, and how we can stop killing each other in the hood with our tongues and bad intentions in the hood.

Intolerance is ripping the black community and all of society apart constantly. Those who do not fit into a mold in which is preset and shifting for control purposes are found. The major medium of intolerance in the Africa American community is still the tongue. The tongue has been the biggest problem in the hood. It was taught by those who were in control and during the days of slavery. The masses created differentiation by labeling them field and house negroes, and they would be at odds. This gave the master control.

The house negro and the negro in the field, were often at odds, this came about because of jealousy. The field negro had the women, and he had privileges most of the house negros did not have. So the story goes even until this day. Normally, it's something said out of the mouth and the tongue from that day until this day is wreaking havoc in the hood. The most deadly force in the black community and the most celebrated weapon in the hood is the tongue. Simon used this beast called the pink tornado to pull this sister down. The tongue is the only power that some people have, and they use it with precision to implode their own community. The tongue alone does not kill however the Bible says it is motivated by Envy. The *Bible* says in Proverbs 3:31: "Envy not the oppressor and choose none of his ways." When the slave begins to envy his master, and when given an opportunity, the slave will be just like the master over other others, but this gives him authority, pride and selfishness. The repetition of belittling others verbally have become so habitual, until it becomes self-hate. This action often repeated day after day month after month week after week and it's inconceivable that reversing this negative trend and entrenched psychologically for over 400 years. reversed this curse in one day a week or a month Psychologically is just about inconceivable, this is done through habit, and habits are done through repetition.

The stress and the repetition of habits normally takes 30 days to establish. It then becomes conditional; it is said, that I thought to paint a word—a word-painting act—and I could become a habit. Habit becomes a lifestyle. So the tongue—as small as it may be—according to the *Bible*, is one of our greatest enemies to self and to any society. But tongue is often misused poorly in the hood. In short, African Americans have been bushwhacked by Post Traumatic Slave Disorder (PTSD), which, at the least, can cause intolerance and unforgiveness in the community.

The catalyst to this thing is dependency. Let me educate you if you please bear with me and say for instance I control it country, in order to maintain control I must control language, so I will give you a Master's degree. I will give you a Bachelor's degree. I will give you a Ph.D. I will give you a vocabulary that is out of this world to make you seem as though you're intelligent. But at the end of the day, you're still an uneducated fool because I control all of society. Oh, you may think you are in control, but the powers-that-be are in "absolute" control.

Everyone especially the African Americans use the tongue more than anything else. It has power because we feel powerless in community, the tongue seemingly giving one power. in the world and society, and so we turn on each other like ravenous dogs. The tongue has become the enemy within. In Ephesians 6 and 12, it says that the *Bible* recognizes that there existed a battle between flesh and blood. We wrestle against principalities in high places. As stated in Proverbs 3:31,

Many African American choose to be the oppressor because African Americans want to be somebody else. African Americans do no think like themselves, but to be the society in which they live.

American Idol is an example of someone wanting to be like somebody else. If most African-Americans would think of what the Bible says, they can reverse this curse. The *Bible* says that before you were formed in your mother's womb, He gave you your gifts. Everything you have is at your disposal, God gave to you before you were born. He even gave you that beautiful dark-brown skin. Here Is one of the greatest stress relievers known to mankind, Your reply to someone who doesn't like the color of your skin is that... ask them this question, have you talked to God as to why he made me like this. He gave me this beautiful tan. I love my tan, man, and feel good about it." Instead of cursing God and wishing you were not born that way, encourage others to embrace what God has given them. Some people in life don't realize why they're here so naturally they go into the opposite directions of discouragement. Some have only an evil mind of shame and disgrace. Remember what the *Bible* says in John 10:10: "The thief comes not but to steal to kill and destroy but Jesus come that you might have life and have it more abundantly." You have everything you need, so don't let someone's tongue affect you.

Back in the 1960s when African Americans came into integration many soon discovered that it was one of the biggest tricks going. That was because it covered segregation. Segregation never went away, and African Americans as a people, put full dependency on the system and Many took their eyes off God. The same God who bought them through though the lynchings and the hard times of life, but many put then and today full dependency on the system because the system said, "I got the money. I got cars. I got things, and you can be just like me." So many African Americans wanted to be like the

Anglo-Saxon - to have things and stuff - but taking my eyes off the prize, which is the Promised Land. When African American put God on the backburner, everything begins to fall apart. Here in this year 2018, African Americans realize they are still a population control which has not changed much in the last 50 years from 13 percent to 15 percent. There is a check and balance system happening to African American in control. The *Bible* says in Matthew 6:23: "Seek ye first the kingdom of heaven and his righteousness and all these things shall be given to you." That's the problem that Many African Americans have now. That's why many use the tongue to kill one another. Come now. Let us study the tongue.

You have just witnessed an actual account about the exciting incident in the hood with Jesus and the prostitute. In context, yes, Simon displayed his bad side. And even as you read this, others in the hood today are practicing the same infectious disease with the tongue. They have been Simonized with a bad case of C.R.A.B.S. That's the couse of so much murder and killing in the hood.

You hit it right on the nail that the tongue is a contributing factor physical violence in the hood it is the root of a whole lot of killing in the hood.

Before we study the tongue, let's discuss the purpose for why you, myself and all humans on the planet earth are here —to glorify God. Ecclesiastes 12:13 states, "For the whole duty of man is to fear God and keep his commandments." Not only were you born with that duty built into you being, but you came equipped. Jeremiah 1:5 says, "Before I formed you in the womb I knew you, before you were born I set you apart; I appointed you as a prophet to the Nations." So you see, you're fearfully and wonderfully made by our Heavenly Father, and you have His gifts to do his duty. Let's begin the process.

Micah 6:8 states: "He has shown thee, old man, what is good; and what does the Lord require of their, but to do justly, and to love mercy, and to walk humbly with thy God?" As we go forward in our study, let us remember not to have a bad case of "Simonitis," which is a bad case of C.R.AB.S: that is, Cognitive Retrogressions Affecting the Black Society, also known as PTSD, Post-Traumatic Slave Disorder. A hint to the wise is sufficient.

Below are ways on how not to be infected.

A. An evil reports distort facts and have incomplete facts of false information. No part of this is to be given or forwarded.
B. The pink tornadoes, the tongue reports, are so destructive that they can even destroy long-lasting close friendshisp. The *Bible* says that whispering separates chief friends (Proverbs 16:28).
C. The tongue is a fire. This is a world of iniquity. It can defile the whole body and set it on fire, that is the course of nature, and it is set on the fire of hell (James 3:6).
D. The whisperer is one who secretly or privately passes an evil report to others (see Psalm 41:7).
E. Gossip: one who magnifies and sensationalizes rumors and partial information.
F. Slanderer: one who seeks to destroy another's credibility or reputation with damaging facts, distortionary effects, or evil suspicions (Numbers 14:36).
G. Busybody: one who digs up evil reports and makes it his business to spread them by means of gossip or slander. (This person is also called a mummy hunter digging up the dead.)

How can you detect a diseased carrier of an evil report? This person will test your spirit before giving you an evil report. Any evidence of a compatible spirit and you will encourage him to give the report. Thus, the disease spreads. The Bible says guard your heart: "Above all else, guard your heart for it is the wellspring of life" (Proverbs 4:23). This disease usually checks your acceptance of his/her report before giving it to you. The person may do this by asking your opinion about a person or will drop a negative comment will then observe your response to it. Be careful. You could be killing somebody. It's called bloodless murder.

A disease carrier will get you to ask for the evil report by creating curiosity for it. Some starters have you hear the person. 'Wait until I tell you about the person,' and so on and so forth. Don't fall for it. You are committing a sin before God. Also, a disease carrier may communicate and report by asking you for counseling about sharing a concern for the person involved. Don't do this.

So, remember next time someone may wants to bring you some disease, you don't need it. It begins with ignorance of what motivates an evil report. See James 3:14–18 for a bitter reaction of personal hurt, rebellion, pride and envy. It's one of Satan's master plans, so don't be Simonized. Remember this.

Shut Up

You make it through this world, but it will be slow.
If you listen to all that is said as you go
You'll be worried and fret and be kept in a stew
What meddlesome tongues must have something to do.
People talk, you know.
If too quiet and noble, they'll have it presumed
That your humble position is only assumed.
You're a wolf in sheep's clothing, or you are a fool.
Don't let this worry you; keep your cool.
People will talk, you know.
If quiet and modest, they'll vent their spleen.
You'd heard some loud hints that you're selfish and mean.
If upright and honest and fair as the day,
They'll call you a rogue in some sly sneaking way.
People will talk, you know.
And if you show the least boldness of heart
Or a slight inclination to take your own part,
They'll call you an upstart, conceited, or vain.
But keep straight ahead; don't stop to explain.
People will talk, you know.
If threadbare your coat, old fashioned your hat,
Someone of course will take notice of that
And hint rather strong that you can't pay your way.
But don't get excited whatever they say
'Cause people will talk, you know.
If you dress in the fashion, doing things to escape
'Cause they'll criticize them in a different shape.
You're ahead of your means or the Taylors unpaid.

Mind your own business, there's naught to be said.
People will talk, you know.
Now the best thing to do is to do as you please.
Then your mind (if you have one) will then be at ease.
Of course, you'll be met with all sorts of abuse,
But don't try to stop them, it'll be of no use
'Cause People will talk, you know.

"The Letter of Necessity for Those in the Hood"

People of color, I greet you in the year of Our Lord, 2018, in the desert of America and the Oasis of the presence. We are in deep appreciation for you and your nation, kindred, clan, tribe and tongues; indeed, you are the survivors of the world's greatest holocaust, which is presently ongoing. Just standing in your presence and numbered with you humbles me and other God-fearing saints as we are continuing in this struggle. In the struggle, we must always remember that the "Promised Land" is not this land, but in Yonder Kingdom to come. Daily, we are to give our heavenly Father the glory and the honor, for He is truly good. He is giving us the ability to endure the hardships and the blessings of life, and hath brought us this far by faith.

I am here to help you solve one of the most complex problems which slavery and oppression has severely imposed upon many people of color in America. This devastating problem has reached a huge portion of our society, nearly wiping out whole generations until it has become the Enemy Within. Tearfully, some of us know it as PTSD, or Post-Traumatic Slave Disorder, which has activated the C.R.A.B.S: Cognitive Retrogressions Affecting the Black Society.

As a people, we are seeing an implosion-factor of choreographed murder at such an enormous rate that it is officially internal genocide.

How did this happen? It's calculated! The process is found in my book, *The Religion of Greed and Its Impact on African Americans.* Read this book for content only. Years ago, Carter G. Woodson wrote *The Mis-Education of the Negro,* in which he argued that although education is for the Negro was a good and necessary thing, they were still dependent on the system for identification and survival. Dr. Woodson traveled the world to find and tell the true and valid story of people of color because the history books were slanted, and not in their favor. This is still profoundly true today. Ponder for a moment: if I treated you bad, why would I teach you the truth about your history – your identity? Think about it. A bachelor's degree, a master's degree and a Ph.D.: your dependence is still on those who are in control of society. I call it "the educated fool syndrome" because many people of color have a vocabulary which is creating a greater separation amongst the classes in the secular world. Now, one can have a vocabulary bigger than a freight train, but mentally, you are still internally dependent upon the system for sustenance. In short, one can be JUST AS happy as a runaway slave, but some continue go back to "Massa" to survive. How cruel!

NOTE: The biggest slave master in the United States is student loans.

NOTE: The highest education one can obtain is a study of God's word daily. Amen!

The intention of this letter is to give you an opportunity to STOP THE KILLING IN THE HOOD! At some point in our lives, you and I have both experienced the impact of death in the hood. You must realize that this is a learned behavior ushered in by slavery and cruel assimilation, which made it so gruesome. The very process of assimilation has caused so many of our people to lose their cultural identity. In the HOOD, the process of assimilation promotes character-killing, social degradation, physical and mental abuse and, of course, fighting among ourselves, which leads to murder. These types of genocides are encouraged and sanctioned by the court system for continual dominance and control. Many people of color live in constant fear and depend on the social system which does not teach real success. They do not know what's going to happen between today and tomorrow. Real success begins with having a relationship with the Lord, thanking Him daily.

People of color, you have been set up and prepared daily to be America's renewable cash crop and cash cows. For years, you have suffered from low personal self-esteem, self-expectancy, self-motivation, self-control, self-discipline and disdain by one another. We are imprisoned more than other ethnic groups/cultures, our health is secondary to research about diseases that impact our community and we are still the lowest poverty group in America: we are menial workers. I suggest you read and study your own history and how we were rulers of the world at one time; this is *paramount* to your understanding. Open your *Bible* to the Book of Genesis and study your history that is your "Missing Link." Study World History and Bible History. Eureka! Your eyes will be opened.

Let me give you a case in point: today's secular media - ABC, NBC and CBS - that is, the American Broadcasting Caucasian, the National Broadcasting Caucasian and the Caucasian Broadcasting Station. Remember President Barack Obama, President of the United States? Ninety-nine percent of the time, the media referred to him as Obama or Mr. Obama. I even heard some black preachers also refer to him as such from the pulpit: Obama, instead of President Obama. And some of our people practiced this same type of slave mentality by referring to President Obama as just Obama. Isn't this amazing? It is an example of the disdain, belittling and wickedness by the press and many of our own people.

America now misses this good-natured person and his great family, but most importantly, his superior leadership skills, his common courtesy, his decency and respect, which they will never be able to erase from the history books. With this new administration, every word that comes out in the media begins with "President." This shows the blatant disrespect for President Obama, and favoritism towards Trump.

The United States was built with the blood, sweat and tears of our forefathers whose minds were seared by the scorching sun and lashed by the "Massa's" whip. The fact is, the whole economy of the United States was built on the backs of slaves; many banks and institutions today are still thriving from the economic and social impact of slavery. The historical fact that many inventions and achievements by our people were and are still being stolen for the sake of greed is appalling and disheartening. Let me not continue to elaborate on our problems, but rather, let's develop the God-given gifts inside of us so that we can be true emancipators; thus, the process begins now. God has not brought us this far to leave us, for He is the God of the oppressed.

I have found a few simple and foolproof methods of getting rid of the cognitive retrogression affecting the black society - the C.R.A.B.S. and Post-Traumatic Slave Disorder, which has been in instilled into people of color for over 400 years. I guarantee that the methods are simple and can be used by any member of your family. These methods are found in the *Bible;* according to Psalms 139:14, we are fearfully and wonderfully made. Although we have distinct differences and similarities, the most important step for this process to begin is to apply a simple act of appreciation. When God made each individual, he made us differently and we should appreciate all of God's creations.

NOTE: The oppressor, the enemy of your very soul, uses fear, stress, envy and dependency as a whip. To the contrary, we must put our dependency in and on God Alone. It will then be easy to forgive and to trust others. Have respect for God by not killing, but by word or through deed.

Practice adulation by esteeming others more so than yourself (Philippians 2 & 3). It is of the up most importance to the survivability of our people. Once this act is in motion, the clutches of the C.R.A.B.S and Post-Traumatic Slave Disorder will dissipate; yes, we can rid ourselves of these two curses which have caused so much Killing In The Hood....

Thus, upon reading this book, we the descendants of slaves, once action is in place, will become self-refueling and self-regenerating for hundreds, maybe thousands of years as the destructive forces of killing others and self dissipates. Remember, "I can do all things through Christ who strengthens me" (Philippians 4:13).

Always remember to appreciate and love others, and to hold onto God's unchanging hand; young soul-brothers must respect the older soul brothers, and older soul-brothers must appreciate the younger soul-brothers. The light-skinned brothers are to appreciate the dark-skinned brothers; the lovely soul-sisters are to love one another. Daily practice of appreciation as well as putting our full dependency in and upon God is required. In this relationship, love, trust and respect Him; then, and only then, will it be easy for us to get rid of the C.R.A.B.S. and the PTSD in the hood.

People of color, this plan is guaranteed by the Living God; once we intentionally practice this method for one year, the slave mentality will dissipate. We must never miss an opportunity to appreciate others, encourage one another, see the good in people - even unkind people; smile and do all the good you can. Then, we, as a people, will emerge as professionally trustworthy and obedient to the Living God and we shall Excel!

Since we are all up in the hood and a lot of us are practicing with precision the destructive traits of Simon (that's running our mouths with hurtful or wrong intentions), here you have a golden opportunity to reverse this curse and be more loving like Jesus in the hood. Jesus' family was from the hood according to the Book of Matthew, the first chapter, and a lot of them had issues. But this mixed multitude reversed the curse and came to Jesus for the cure. Jesus was from the hood. This is the true color of Jesus. His color is love, which enables one to appreciate everyone and everything (John 13:1). What color was Jesus? His color is joy. Jesus' color is peace. Jesus' color is patience. His color in the hood is kindness, goodness, faithfulness and gentleness. The color of Jesus is compassion. What color was Jesus? His color was thoughtfulness and discretion.

That is the quality or behavior of speaking in such a way as to avoid causing offense or revealing private information. What color was Jesus in the hood? He was all this and so much more. It was his color of purity and holiness. What color was Jesus? His color was friendship, honesty and truthfulness. His color was dependable. His color was having gratitude and contentment and pure, down-to-earth generosity. What color was Jesus in the hood or wherever you are? It's confidence and encouragement. What color was Jesus? His color was being optimistic to think the best of and to be positive with people in all situations.

You will find this in Romans 8 and the 25th verse in Romans 28. What color was Jesus? He was the right reverend according to Psalm 1:11 and 9. What color was Jesus? He was being a good example, not allowing His relationship with God, His father, to become hypocritical as your relationship with Him should not be hypocritical. That's the color of Jesus in the hood. What color was Jesus? His color is dependable. His color i determination, and that is the ability to make the difficult decision and accomplish God's work based on the truth in God's Word regardless of the opposition (Psalm 119:30 and 2 Timothy 4:7–8).

What color was Jesus? His color is devotion. The color of Jesus is discernment. The color of Jesus is discrete. The color of Jesus is discipline. The color of Jesus in the hood is having endurance. The color of Jesus is being fearless. The color of Jesus is being godly and having grace. Jesus's color is having and being harmless, being honest and hospitable, just doing what is right, impartial in right, according to God's will (Genesis 6:9). Yes, my friend, in the hood, you'll find that Jesus's color was loyalty to remain committed to those things that God had placed before him to do. And you should be loyal also after you receive the Holy Spirit. What color was Jesus? It is strength under control, personal rights, and expectations to God our Father (Psalm 62 and 5). That's the color of Jesus.

What color was Jesus? He was merciful. He was patient. He had perseverance. He was prompt and prudent. All these are the colors of Jesus and so much more. What color was Jesus in the hood? What color is Jesus today? His color is respectable. The color of Jesus is security and submissiveness. The color of Jesus is truth and the light of the world. The color of Jesus, my friends, is understanding and virtuous. The color of Jesus is zealous (John 8:29). This is the color of Jesus in the hood. Let the church say, amen.

Intro to the Workshop

According to some research, traditional habits are formed from repetition. The stress and repetition is reinforced to happen usually after 30 days of a constant, learned habit. And it's yours that a habit becomes real and is automatically turned into action—action overtime and stir confusion on the thread of life. If instituted, it will reassure a long-term happening. In fact, the heaven is moved to a priority for survival of thought to those in the victim's environment. If the habit is reinforced to degrade the victim and constantly remind the victim that he/she is nothing as a human being and equal to or lower than an animal that has been physically abused, then it becomes a stable way of life, and it is almost impossible to get rid of.

My second case in point is the Stockholm syndrome. One may be the victim that begins to love the power of his master and to identify with him when given the opportunity. He/ her will lash out at herself because of the instilled self-hate imposed by the oppressor. Therefore, those who look like the victim will be the internal oppression and repeat the same process of creating self-hatred and oppression. Actions, in some cases, are as follows: physical abuse, mental abuse, constant suspicions, mistrust and murder, both verbally and physically.

As in many cases, the system will give this person little or no big time. The system is all about constant genocide following the rape of a woman with medium sentencing in 1990—a white woman with a ten-year sentence. It has been in equipment for five years, a black woman two years. See the statistics in which we produced only 1 percent of population growth by the year 2015. There is a reason why these statistics stand. I have been a victim of an internal munching. What about my character being put into question? And until this day, the question still exists, though there is no foundation for the question.

Generally, some of them who are authority figures who have become educated fools strike out in this manner to maintain control and just to say, "I'm in charge." The head-negro-in-charge syndrome perpetuate internal racism (witchcraft) Witchcraft is nothing but pure hate and a stench in the nostrils of God. Oppressed people oppress those people that are under them; oftentimes, it is black on black. Compressions and oppressions have been impacted by the impressions of having pressures in the family, wife, children even friends. Implosion happens sometimes is often the outcome due to the inability to tap into God-created abilities to reverse the curse.

People normally make choices, and that's when things get a little tricky if they don't have God in their lives. By having control over the mechanisms of jobs and only giving a few jobs, plus human nature, life must go on. Some children go into a killing spree because they do not have self-worth, putting their dependency on a system that is brutal. It is better to put your trust in God and lean not to your own understanding. In all your ways, acknowledge him, and he will direct your path.

Not depending on God is a cause of low self-esteem and low-self-direction, and every other thing that they became in these days is a movement of resentment. It is in these days that the movement is taught by this society.

The process of C.R.A.B.S and the Post-Traumatic Slave Disorder is wreaking havoc on the black community. We just do it. Many people of color do not trust and do not appreciate one another, and, thus, have no expectations of one another. The C.R.A.B.S and the PTSD is a direct derivative of institutionalized racism, what's called the "rippling effect."

Long ago, and when this nation was first formed, racism(witchcraft on steroids) there exists a battle between the flesh and blood. We wrestle not against principalities in high places as stated in Ephesians 6:12. This issue of witchcraft is real. It's a real issue and will be here until Jesus returns.

People of color would never be able to destroy the fat enemy called PTSD until they are able to identify the enemy. The *Bible* says in Proverbs 3:31, "In did not build pressure and choose none of his way." The word *jealous* is often used in reference to God, saying, "I am a jealous God." So many oppressed people and people of color are jealous of the oppressor to the point that they want to be just like the oppressor. When they become jealous of the oppressor, they begin to act like the oppressor. When people of color are envious and jealous of your person, your present does not need to be there. In the schools, African American people are prevented from learning because African American children in the present choose their way. The African American child will go to school and learn to read and write because of the enemy that's on the inside.

Internal hate and internal distrust—all these mechanisms were put here for control in the astonishment that we were an asset in this country. During the slavery, we comprised 20% of the population. That's when we were an asset. Soon after the Emancipation

Proclamation, freedom was obtained by a lot of people of color. The population decreased now these days to 14 percent to 13 percent. Now we are a liability in this country. Internal conflict, which has always been present, has taught people of color that they cannot perform and taught them to have low expectations of themselves. So they dump drugs into the black community and make the warlords kill us. That's the new Klansman.

The reason is the police will not arrest a man for bringing tons of drugs into your community for the oppressed. The aspect of putting you in jail for using drugs is that it continues with more genocide. Case in point, all in the North, there were drugs on the streets of America. Him and George W. Bush, Sr.—neither one went to jail for killing black folks by the dozen to sponsor the Iran-Contra War. I was fortunate enough some years later to assist in North stunning defeat as part of the sixty-four-man coalition. When North ran for senate here in the Commonwealth of Virginia. North had 25 million dollars in his war chest, Chuck Rob had only 5 million dollars, yet we defeated him with good old groundwork. I'm proud to be one of the sixty-four-man coalition that defeated that Rascal.

This message applies not only to people of color, but also to anyone else. Also, it's about oppression. It is about internal racism. It is about manifest destiny. Right now, that's what some folks have declared to rule no matter what the outcome or circumstances.

Since Jesus was down in the hood, He gave African Americans the answers for how to destroy the enemy that have caused so much destruction in neck of the woods, in the hood. First, Jesus tells African Americans to change there focus to what the *Bible* says, and not the oppressor in the hood. Know that anywhere else, focus on God and God only, as we begin the process of destroying the enemy within in the hood.

African Americans are to take there values from God, not from the oppressor. The value of this land is not money. Don't put your dependency on cars, homes, moneys and cars. The *Bible* says in Matthew 6:33, "But seek ye first the kingdom of God and his righteousness and all these other things shall be added unto you." And when you get those things, use it to glorify God.

The very basics of studies for African Americans are people of color in the hood. Stop the killing. It begins in the Book of Psalm and then in the Book of Proverbs. Read slowly for one solid month these two books alone to understand who the shepherd is, who God is, and what His intentions are for you—to live for Him. You'll find that in the book of Micah 6 and 8, it says to justly love and have mercy. That is the only thing that we can do.

The *Bible* says also in Ecclesiastes that the only thing man can do is to fear God and keep His commandments. Let's start a revolution in the hood—a revolution of reading God's Word and abiding by these Words daily—and the killing will subside.

Jesus today and Simon are on a rampage. We still have some Simons in the hood still wreaking havoc, still raising hell and still getting down on people. Let's reverse this curse. Jesus was down in the hood to try to undo some of the things that were no good that someone had placed in his face. You and I, let's reverse the curse of Simon and stop the killing in the hood.

Let's begin a campaign today to get rid of mudslingers ananumas, loose-lip Susies and some lying lollies. Speaking of lies, one of the most incredible things that we teach and I have been taught is how to be intolerant of ourselves but tolerant of others who rule over us in this society. This intolerance is ripping the black neighborhoods in the hood apart culturally with indifference. But we should appreciate one another because God made us in His image. Intolerance is consistent with pride, cultural differences, statuses, social structure, outlandish crazy ideas, and superiority. In Christ, there is no bonded or free or Greek. We are all one in Christ Jesus.

What happened is that when the captors captured their victims and enslaved them, for maintaining control. The captors had to reassure internal conflict in the persons they had enslaved. One of the ways to keep a person enslaved is to give them half the truth. One of the half truths given to the slaves in America is Ephesians 6 and 5: "Servants, be obedient to them that are your Masters according to the flesh, with fear and trembling, and singleness of heart as unto Christ." What is not given to the slaves is that they must be conditionally treated as humans and also give to the slave masters the content that the masters have under rule of law also.

Intolerance has also taught us how we should be a bigoted in the hood.

"You know, I'm better than you."

"I wish."

"I close."

"I have a regular."

"I pray."

"It's all about me."

I'm telling you that God does not like selfish individuals. It just happens in the hood. It's a part of intolerance. However, the *Bible* says that God loves those who are humble. God is merciful. To be a sinner is with the center cry it out, and social weight.

The disease of gossip and slander is the most crippling disease in America, especially in the hood. Slander and gossip are diseases that eat away at the very heart and soul of a community It is very difficult for the people to be farsighted enough to realize what will happen in the future after his lies have actually destroyed an individual.

Gossip is no different than stealing; in fact, it is worse than stealing. It is actually murder. You see, after the person's dignity has been destroyed and he's been cleared of the accusation, the damage is irreversible.

However, those who stand on principle are always under the threshing of the tongue from those who are weak and spineless. Perhaps you have seen some Simon in your lifetime with those cognitive jawbones and slack-minded people. The *Bible* says that if any man among you seem to be religious but not by his tongue, this man's religion ain't worth $0.02 at all.

Here are some ways to protect yourself from the tongue:

1) Put up a No Trespassing sign on yourself and on your families. Pray without ceasing that no one is to say anything evil against you and your family and those whom you love.
2) Walk away from those who seem to want to do harm to others. That is a fallacious prevarication, and that's a bad lie.
3) Avoid people who curse and use foul language. This is caustic to your very soul.
4) Do not listen to negativities about anything. Be positive at all times.
5) Appreciate people from all walks of life.

Maintain an open opinion of yourself, and think positive all the time. You will live and stay alive for a long time as you walk away from the claws of the C.R.A.B.S and the PTSD.

Because of the implosion factor introduced in slavery into the black community. Things have replaced humans. The newfound religion of the greed of things is more valuable than the relationship with God. Since the 1960s, when African Americans were duped into believing that things and stuff could supersede what God had planned for us to worship Him and Him alone. But, many African Americans began to worship things and stuff. Year 2000s, many African Americans are worse off now than in the 1960s. The miseducators will give you an education. They will give you a Bachelor's Degree, they will give you a Master's degree, they will give you a Ph.D. and they will give you a vocabulary as big as a house. But you still must put your dependency on the miseducators.

The major tool in the hood that costs so much destruction is the tongue. The *act* is considered bloodless murder, which leads to real murder. This thing called the C.R.A.B.S has toppled governmenst, wrecked marriages, ruined characters and careers and first reputations, and caused headaches, nightmares, indigestion and stupid suspicions. It has generated grief and dispatched innocent people to cry on that pillow. It is called gossip and slander. It makes headlines and headaches. So before you repeat a story, ask yourself if it is true. If it is a little sensitive, shut up!

The following is a poem by an unknown author that I wish to share with you. Maybe we can get rid of some Simons in the hood if they pay attention to this point. You may get through this world but will be slow.

If you listen to all that is said as you go
UB word and fretted to keep in the

The weapon of mass destruction, the C.R.A.B.S, the PTSD, or whatever you may call it. The tongue is one bad motorcycle in the hood. It's a character assassinator. And it's so universal because no one seriously believes that they are at fault no matter how wrong they are. The struggle for the minds of Americans, especially in the hood, is taking place in the most religious places and in political circles.

There has been a tendency on the part of anybody that has stood for social justice throughout history (and in the present) to hold no exception to the rule, with the mass media that tongue in the pink tornado.

Gossip and slander are crippling diseases in America. By the way, that thing you call racism in America is not really something new. The *Bible* calls it wickedness, which is actually nothing but good old-fashioned witchcraft. And the witches and warlocks are having themselves a ball in America, pointing fingers at people who are ethnically different than they are, saying that they are inferior. Witchcraft in America is the new religion, but the witchcraft in the hood is even worse. It's because we practice how to kill, maim, destroy and corrupt in the hood.

Let's begin to reverse this curse.

Index

H

I

J

K

L

M

N

O

P

R

S

Lightning Source UK Ltd.
Milton Keynes UK
UKHW040601021218
333216UK00002B/33/P